YOUR LAND AND MY LAND
The Middle East

We Visit

YEMEN

Claire

O'Neal

Mitchell Lane
PUBLISHERS
P.O. Box 196
Hockessin, Delaware 19707

YOUR LAND
AND
MY LAND
The Middle
East

Afghanistan
Iran
Iraq
Israel
Kuwait
Oman
Pakistan
Saudi Arabia
Turkey
Yemen

KIRKUK
ZAGROS MOUNTA
Qom
Arāk
Kermānshāh
Eşfahān
Baghdad
IRAQ
IRAN

YOUR LAND
AND
MY LAND
The Middle
East

We Visit

YEMEN

Sanaa
YEMEN
Al
udaydah
Al Mukallā
Arabia

TASCO

Printing   1   2   3   4   5   6   7   8   9

Library of Congress Cataloging-in-Publication Data
O'Neal, Claire.
We visit Yemen / by Claire O'Neal.
p. cm. — (Your land and my land: the Middle East)
Includes bibliographical references and index.
ISBN 978-1-58415-961-2 (library bound)
1. Yemen (Republic)—Juvenile literature. I. Title.
DS247.Y48O54 2012
953.3—dc23
                                                                                                    2011016773
eBook ISBN: 9781612281063

PUBLISHER'S NOTE: This story is based on the author's extensive research, which she believes to be accurate. Documentation of this research is on page 60.

The Internet sites referenced herein were active as of the publication date. Due to the fleeting nature of some web sites, we cannot guarantee they will all be active when you are reading this book.

To reflect current usage, we have chosen to use the secular era designations BCE ("before the common era") and CE ("of the common era") instead of the traditional designations BC ("before Christ") and AD (*anno Domini,* "in the year of the Lord").

j953.3
ONE

Contents

Introduction

Since the dawn of civilization, the Middle East has been a crossroads for trade, culture, and knowledge. Known as the "cradle of civilization," people have lived, fought, and worshiped there for millennia. Though many Middle Eastern nations share the Arabic language, heritage, and Islamic religion, they do not always get along. Today the Middle East makes headlines almost daily, with news of oil supplies, wealthy kings, Islamic extremists, and civil and international warfare.

Many Middle Eastern countries sit on the Arabian Peninsula. This vast rectangle of land, while mostly desert, boasts the birthplace of three major world religions: Islam, Christianity, and Judaism. The peninsula is also the world's largest source of oil and natural gas. Its importance in the world economy—and sometimes its political instability—can outshine its beauty and rich cultural history. Yemen occupies the southwest corner of the Arabian Peninsula, on the Gulf of Aden

between the Red Sea and the Arabian Sea. This ruggedly beautiful "Roof of Arabia" uses its highlands to keep out invaders and insulate its people's ancient ways.

An elderly Yemeni man greets a visitor from his front door in Sana'a. Like most Yemeni men, he wears a sportcoat over a white robe called a *thawb*. A favorite accessory of Yemeni men is the *jambiya*, a traditional curved dagger with a carved handle made of bone or ivory.

Yemen, Ancient and Beautiful

In Yemen there's an old joke. The angel Gabriel took God on a whirlwind tour of modern-day Earth. They flew over Europe. Gabriel pointed down. "London is to your left. There's Paris, on your right." God scratched his head, puzzled. "I don't recognize a thing." They flew over the Arabian Peninsula, and God nodded in approval. "Finally! Yemen! It looks exactly the same."[1]

Traveling to Yemen feels like taking a trip through time, a rare opportunity to see the world and its people as they may have existed thousands of years ago. In this ancient land, most people live as they have for centuries. Conveniences such as computers, shopping malls, and even flushing toilets are rare. On average, one Yemeni out of 100 has access to the Internet.[2] Certainly, large cities such as the capital, Sana'a, and the port city of Aden have many modern amenities, including running water, cell phones, Internet access, and shopping malls, but even they boast homes older than the United States. At souks—colorful open-air marketplaces—vendors peddle groceries, spices, cloth, and goods exactly as their ancestors did for generations. Yemeni men proudly walk with *jambiya*—fancy curved daggers—at their belts, seemingly ready to defend their honor at a moment's notice. Their wives and daughters drape themselves in abayas, black robes that float around their bodies like fluttering butterflies.

Most Yemenis live in small mountain villages perched on hillsides, farming goats, sheep, and vegetables as their ancestors have done for centuries, sometimes without running water or electricity. The wild, rugged mountains bring a forced though welcome isolation. Where the construction of roads is nearly impossible, embracing modern ways just doesn't make sense. Yemenis enjoy the closeness of their families and the company of friends and guests.

However, forces from within threaten to destroy the ancient beauty of this country. Yemenis struggle with widespread unemployment, poverty, and poor nutrition. Many believe the corrupt government, led

Satellite dishes adorn centuries-old houses made of mud brick and gypsum in the city of Sana'a.

by President Ali Abdullah Saleh since 1978, is more concerned with keeping control than helping its people. Terrorist threats by al-Qaeda and Houthi rebels have made travel unsafe in the north and west and destroyed thousands of homes. Yemen today stands at a crossroads, determined to preserve its ancient values while struggling to bring peace, health, and jobs to its people. Can this ancient land find its place in the modern world?

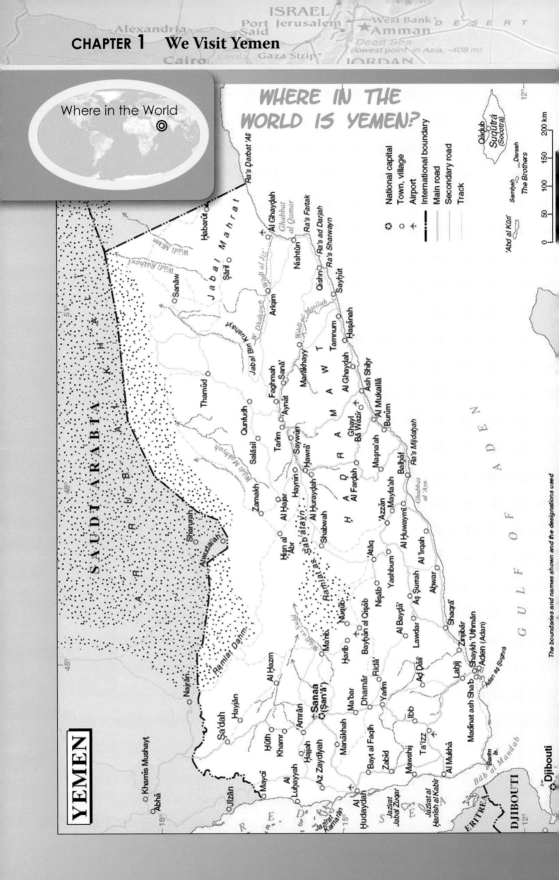

Where in the World ◎

WHERE IN THE WORLD IS YEMEN?

YEMEN FACTS AT A GLANCE

Country Name: Republic of Yemen

Founded: May 22, 1990

Population: 24,133,492 (July 2011 estimate)

Area: 203,850 square miles (527,968 square kilometers), about twice the size of Wyoming

Highest elevation: 12,336 feet (3,760 meters), at Jabal an-Nabi Shu'ayb

Lowest elevation: sea level, along the coast

Capital city: Sana'a

Other major cities: Aden, Mukallah, Al-Hudaydah, Ta'izz, Ibb

Form of government: Constitutional republic (president, vice president, and prime minister)

Governates: 21

Official language: Arabic

Official religion: Islam; major sects are Zaydi (Shi'a) and Shafi'i (Sunni)

Currency: Yemeni rial

National motto: *Allah, al-Watan, ath-Thawra, al-Wahdah* (God, nation, revolution, unity)

National anthem: "United Republic"

Flag: Three horizontal stripes of red, white, and black, colors chosen from the Arab Liberation flag. They represent a dark past (black), a bright future (white), and blood shed for unity (red).

National bird: Golden-winged grosbeak (*Rhynchostruthus socotranus*)

National flower: Jebel Iraf Aloe (*Aloe irafensis*)

National mammal: Arabian leopard (*Panthera pardus nimr*)

National tree: Dragon's Blood tree (*Dracaena cinnabari*)

Sources: U.S. Central Intelligence Agency *World Factbook*: "Yemen"
   https://www.cia.gov/library/publications/the-world-factbook/geos/ym.html
"Yemen Names National Bird," *BirdLife International*, July 3, 2008.
   http://www.birdlife.org/news/news/2008/07/yemens_national_bird.html

Yemen chameleon

Solomon, King of Israel, receives the Queen of Sheba in this painting by Flemish master Frans Francken II (1581–1642). The wise and respected queen traveled to Jerusalem around the tenth century BCE, bringing gifts for Solomon of gold, jewels, exotic wood, and precious spices from her wealthy domain.

The History of "Arabia Felix"

The Bible and Koran (also spelled Qu'ran) both tell the story of the Great Flood, when God sent forty days and forty nights of rain to cleanse the world. God commanded a faithful man named Noah to build a great ship—an ark—to carry his family and Earth's living creatures over the floodwaters. When the flood receded, Noah's son, Shem, came down from the mountains where the ark had landed, following a bird sent by God to show him the way home. According to Yemenis, Shem built his home on a rich plain at the foot of Mount Nugum, calling it Madinat Sam, or Shem's City. Shem's City still stands today as Sana'a, the capital of Yemen, the oldest continually inhabited city on Earth. From Sana'a, Shem's descendants, the Semites,

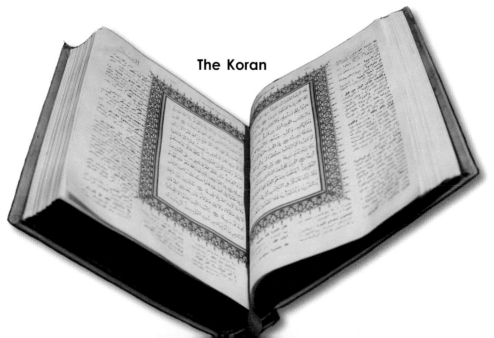

The Koran

would go on to populate Arabia, Africa, and Europe. Their ancient languages evolved into today's Arabic and Hebrew.

Yemen sits at a unique physical crossroads between Africa, Asia, and Europe, home to civilizations for thousands of years. Archaeologists have found stone tools that date the earliest settlements in Hadramawt and Al-Mahwit provinces back to 8000 BCE.[1] Yemenis are taught that the great ruler Qahtan, son of Shem, united the peoples of southern Arabia in the 2000s BCE. Three new kingdoms developed in Yemen around 1000 BCE—Hadramawt in the east, and Qataban and Saba (also called Sheba) in the central highlands. The three kingdoms lived peacefully alongside each other, domesticating the one-humped camel to provide them with meat, milk, and transportation.

During the reign of the three kingdoms, ancient Greek geographer Ptolemy referred to Yemen as "Arabia Felix," meaning "happy" or "lucky Arabia." Among Arab countries, Yemen boasts the most favorable climate for farming valuable crops such as coffee and saffron. Frankincense and myrrh—ingredients for perfumes, incense, and medicines—were especially important to the spice trade. From Egypt to Greece to Rome, ancient civilizations had insatiable appetites for these strongly scented resins, which were harvested as sap from plants that grew only in southern Arabia. At times, frankincense and myrrh were more valuable than gold. These crops were transported by traders who followed snaking camel caravan routes west through the highlands of southern Arabia. Traders made a living—and made Yemen

Old Marib was once the capital of the mighty Sabean kingdom. The desert now preserves its mud-brick ruins.

wealthy—by selling these crops along with eastern luxuries brought from India and China.

Sabeans enjoyed particular influence and prosperity. Bilqis, Queen of Sheba, built up the city of Marib as a great center of trade and industry. Both the Bible and the Koran describe a meeting between Bilqis and King Solomon of Israel in the tenth century BCE, where she is depicted as beautiful, wise, mysterious, and fabulously wealthy.[2] In the eighth century BCE, the Sabeans built the Great Dam of Marib to keep the waters of the Wadi Dhana in the valley, allowing people to farm the Marib Valley. Considered a marvel of engineering in its day, the dam stood until the sixth century CE.[3]

The three kingdoms declined in the first century CE. Arabian caravan routes fell out of favor when Greek navigator Hippalus discovered a sea route from Egypt to India. The Himyarite Empire rose in Yemen along the Red Sea, building ports to supply the sailors. When the Roman Empire embraced Christianity in 323 CE, demand for frankincense and myrrh dwindled, and Yemen's formerly wealthy traders found themselves on hard times.

With little to offer the outside world, Yemenis turned inward, looking for God. Many of them converted from the sun worship of their Sabean ancestors to Christianity and Judaism, which were preached by missionaries from the north between 323 and the 500s CE. Jewish Sabean ruler Yusuf Ashaar Dhu Nuwas declared Judaism the official state religion in the sixth century CE, executing more than 20,000 Christians who refused to convert. This angered the king of

Ethiopia, Abraha of Axum, who conquered Nuwas in 523 and demanded the Sabeans convert to Christianity.

Islam arrived in Yemen in 628 CE, shaping the rest of the country's story. The Prophet Muhammad established the caliphate—a system of religious government—that ruled the Arabian Peninsula from the seventh to the tenth century CE. By the ninth century, however, power in Yemen had shifted to the local Zaydi sect of Shi'ites. The Zaydi sect teaches that it is one's moral duty to overthrow unjust rulers, a view that complicates government and continues to fuel bloody conflicts in the region.

Muhammad preaches to his followers in this painting by Russian Grigory Gagarin (1811–1893). Many fundamentalist Muslims consider depictions of Muhammad as blasphemous, but these depictions were not always forbidden.

From the seventh to the fifteenth century, the caliphs ruling Yemen lived in constant violence, struggling against rebels who opposed their politics. Most caliphs were murdered, often poisoned, by those next in line to rule. The Ottoman Empire squelched the infighting when it conquered the Arabian Peninsula in 1538. Britain, in an effort to protect its shipping interests, occupied the port of Aden from 1839. Between 1901 and 1905, Britain and the Ottomans agreed on a boundary line between their territories; Britain controlled south Yemen as the Aden Protectorate, and the Ottomans claimed the north.

On November 1, 1918, with the Ottoman Empire on the decline, Zaydi imams declared northern independence. They kept the north undeveloped and closed to the outside world. Unhappy citizens led by Colonel Abdullah al-Sallal revolted in 1962, overthrowing the government and creating the Yemen Arab Republic. Almost immediately, a bloody civil war erupted between al-Sallal's forces, backed by Egypt and the Soviet Union, and soldiers loyal to the old imam regime. After several leaders were assassinated, Ali Abdullah Saleh rose to power in 1978. An officer in the army, Saleh became a successful president of the militaristic North Yemen.

Meanwhile, southern Yemenis rebelled against the British, but they had neither the money nor the might to oust them until the 1960s. With help from the Soviet Union, Yemeni rebels formed the National Liberation Front and chased out the British. On November 30, 1967, South Yemen declared independence, naming their new country the People's Republic of Southern Yemen (PRSY). Its name changed to the People's Democratic Republic of Yemen (PDRY) in 1970. Backed by the Soviets, PDRY became the first Communist Arabic state.

Despite conflicting interests between the foreign powers that funded both governments, and doubt among clan leaders that any government could serve them well, the two Yemens wanted to become one. A major motivation was the decline of the Soviet Union, a disaster for the PDRY's economy. Additionally, the discovery of oil in 1980 along the border of the two Yemens provided a potentially rich source of revenue to these poor countries. On May 22, 1990, the two Yemens united to form the Republic of Yemen. The parliaments of both countries elected Saleh as the new president.

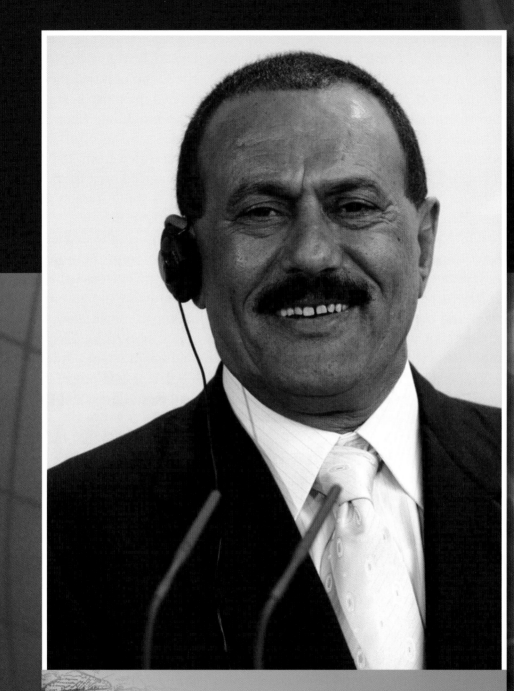

Yemen's president since 1978, Ali Abdullah Saleh has juggled demands from warring sheiks and Islamic terrorists. By 2011, with Yemen's poor economy and standards of living, many Yemenis were crying out for a new leader.

Government

The Republic of Yemen is divided into 21 governorates, or provinces. The country is headed by a president and his appointed prime minister. In 2011, the president was Ali Abdullah Saleh, and the prime minister was Ali Mohammed Majur (also spelled Mujawwar). Laws are made in a bicameral (two-chambered) legislature: an elected Assembly of Representatives with 301 members, and an appointed Shura Council of 111 members.

In 1999, Yemen held its first open presidential elections, a landmark event for democracy in Arabia. President Saleh won 96.2 percent of the vote against Najib Qahtan al-Shabi, the son of the former president of South Yemen.[1] On September 20, 2006, Saleh was reelected as president with 77.2 percent of the vote against opponent Faisal Bin Shamlan, an intellectual and a lifelong Yemeni politician.[2]

Yemen strives to be known as an open and free democracy. However, many Yemenis and outside analysts have accused Saleh of running one of the most corrupt governments in the world. In 1994, rebels in the former South accused Saleh of giving more power and attention to the former North. A civil war broke out, and Saleh's superior military viciously crushed the rebellion. In 2005, Saleh assured the country he would step down as president to allow new leadership. He broke the promise, claiming he felt that the people of Yemen were calling him to run.

Saleh has said that governing Yemen is "like dancing on the heads of snakes."[3] While most Yemenis voted for Saleh, their loyalty has

Yemenis revere Islamic politician Sheik Abdul Majeed al-Zindani, calling him the voice of the Yemeni people. He heads the Muslim Brotherhood in Yemen, a political movement, and also founded and heads Iman University in Yemen.

remained local. Yemenis do not readily allow their government to assert control, especially in isolated mountain villages. Leading families of each clan or community elect leaders called sheiks to settle disputes among families. Naturally, sheiks from mountain villages and those from cities differ in their opinions about what the president should be doing.

The Zaydi clan is one of the richest and most powerful, and it causes the most trouble for Yemen's government. The revolution against North Yemen's imams in 1960 was started, in part, to break up the Zaydis' tight hold on Yemen's fertile land. The Zaydis—a Shi'ite Muslim sect—make up over one-quarter of Yemenis. They deeply distrust the national government, which is mostly Sunni. Zaydis in the northern province of Sa'ada, called Houthis, have had bitter, violent clashes with the government since 2004. The fighting has forced up to 200,000 Yemenis to leave their homes in the north. President Saleh's government accused the Houthis of Iranian support, while the Houthis insisted that Saleh was a puppet of Saudi Arabia. Saleh and rebel leader Abdul Malik Houthi agreed to a cease-fire in the "six years' war" in February 2010 in an effort to make the north safer for villagers to return.

By 2011, Saleh was facing international criticism for al-Qaeda's growing presence in Yemen. Al-Qaeda's infamous leader, Osama bin Laden, had roots there—his father was born in the Wadi Hadramawt region. Al-Qaeda, a militant Islamic group, first gained strength as

Soaring palaces in Sa'ada gave the city its name, which translated means "he who has ascended." Sa'ada has become a hotbed of violence, a center of fighting between the Houthi rebels and government troops.

mujahideen—fighters for Islam—in the 1980s as the world cheered on their fight to keep Soviet forces from occupying Afghanistan. Young Yemenis streamed into Afghanistan to fight alongside their Muslim brothers. After Soviet withdrawal, al-Qaeda fighters were left with millions of dollars' worth of weaponry and bitter feelings toward the West. On October 12, 2000, al-Qaeda operatives bombed the USS *Cole* as it sat in Aden's harbor, killing 17 and injuring 37 U.S. servicemen. One year later, they carried out a similar attack on the French tanker *Limburg*. One of the al-Qaeda hijackers responsible for the September 11, 2001, attack on the Pentagon, Khalid al-Mihdhar, had ties to Yemen. In December 2009, a twenty-three-year-old Nigerian, trained by al-Qaeda in Yemen, tried to detonate a bomb he had smuggled in his underwear onto a flight from Amsterdam to Detroit. And in October 2010, explosives destined for Jewish temples in Chicago were shipped from a UPS facility in Sana'a. Officials feared that Yemen's poverty, corruption, isolation, and weakly enforced laws were making Saleh's backyard a perfect location for new al-Qaeda headquarters.

Protesters nationwide were again demanding Saleh's resignation in the spring of 2011 as unrest swept through the Middle East. Support for Saleh evaporated in May 2011 as his long-time allies Saudi Arabia and the United States urged him to step down and transfer power to his vice president. Many feared that Saleh's refusal to give up his power would lead to civil war.

A village perches in the scenic Haraz Mountains in western Yemen. Farmers cut steps, called terraces, into the mountains to create fields for farming.

Chapter 4

Hot Lands and the Roof of Arabia

Yemen's name means "south" in Arabic—south of Mecca, the spiritual heart of Islam. This rectangular country is bordered on the north and east by land and on the south and west by water. Beyond Yemen's northern border stretch the vast desert and hills of Saudi Arabia. It shares its eastern border with the Sultanate of Oman. Yemen's western coast follows the Red Sea, which separates the Arabian Peninsula from Africa. The Gulf of Aden lines Yemen's southern coast, connecting the Red Sea to the Arabian Sea and the Indian Ocean beyond. The African countries of Djibouti, Eritrea, and Somalia lie across these bodies of water.

Yemen lies at the southern end of the Sarawat Mountains, a range that spans the western Arabian Peninsula and runs parallel to the Red Sea. The tallest peaks and deepest valleys of the Sarawat Mountains are found in Yemen, giving it the nickname "The Roof of Arabia." Highlands make up the landscape of nearly the entire country, bordered along the coasts by narrow plains.

The west coast—known as the Tihama—forms a narrow, sandy plain 15 to 40 miles (24 to 65 kilometers) wide, running north to south.

Blue lizard

Tihama, Yemen

Tihama means "hot lands" for a reason, boasting some of the hottest temperatures in the world. Summer temperatures easily reach highs of 110°F (43°C), with high humidity. Rarely do winter temperatures drop below 65°F (18°C). The region is also technically a desert, receiving an average of 9 inches (23 centimeters) of rain each year. Most Tihamans live in the port city of Al Hudaydah (population 400,000), the birthplace of the coffee trade and the capital of the Tihama province.[1] The Tihama was also once home to the University of Zabid, a world-renowned center of Islamic and scientific learning. Many buildings still stand in the ancient walled city of Zabid, including over 100 mosques.[2] UNESCO named Zabid a World Heritage Site in 1993 to protect the many crumbling ancient buildings that would otherwise be replaced by modern construction.

Zabid

Heading east from the Tihama, cliffs mark the start of the Haraz range of the Sarawat Mountains. The mountains are steepest and most rugged in this western part; rises of 8,200 feet (2,500 meters) are not uncommon. Wind and rapid elevation changes squeeze precipitation out of clouds, yielding the highest rainfall levels in Arabia. The city of Ta'izz, for example, averages 30 inches (76 centimeters) of rainfall annually. Rain comes every month to the province of Ibb—the city of Ibb averages about 40 inches (100 centimeters) of rainfall annually—making the area famous for its fertile farmland.

As the mountains continue east, they flatten into a wide central highland. Most Yemenis live in the central highlands, drawn by the breathtaking scenery, dry air, and mild climate with pleasant seasons. Summertime high temperatures hover near 70°F (21°C), and winter temperatures just reach freezing (32°F/0°C). Yemen's capital and most populated city, Sana'a, lies in the heart of the central highlands, surrounded by tall peaks that include Jabal an-Nabi Shu'ayb (12,336 feet/3,760 meters), the highest point in Yemen. At 7,380 feet (2,249 meters) above sea level, Sana'a is also one of the highest capital cities in the world.

Monsoon rains come to the central highlands in April and May, and then again in June and July, bringing welcome freshwater in a country with no lakes or rivers. The monsoons cause flash floods so heavy that they wear channels called wadis down mountainsides. A wadi—Arabic for "valley"—looks like a dry riverbed for most of the year. However, the most fertile wadis hold water underground throughout the year. Villages form around these fertile wadis, where plants grow in vibrant green ribbons snaking down the otherwise barren mountains. One of the largest and most fertile wadis is Wadi Hadramawt. In Arabic, the name means "death is present," perhaps because of the fleeting nature of the water supply.

1,000-year-old minaret in Jiblah, Ibb

Yemen's northeast is taken over by a desert known as the Rub' al Khali, or Empty Quarter, which stretches into the interior of the Arabian Peninsula. There, droughts that last for five years with no rain at all are common. Daily highs in the summer months can reach 124°F (51°C). If the heat, wind, and lack of water didn't scare off ancient travelers, the Bedouin tribes might have. This group of wandering desert herders does not take kindly to outsiders.

Yemen's coastline has long played an important role in the country's economy. The busy port city of Aden, after which the Gulf of Aden takes its name, has been a popular spot to trade and take on supplies since ancient times. Aden sits near a strait where the Gulf of Aden and the Red Sea meet, where the corner of Yemen and the Horn of Africa lie only 18 miles (29 kilometers) apart from each other. This

strait is known as the Bab el-Mandeb, Arabic for "Gate of Tears." Beyond the strait await the coasts of Sudan, Egypt, Israel, Jordan, and Saudia Arabia, Yemen's neighbor to the north, where Islamic pilgrims still seek Mecca along the Red Sea coast.

The Bab el-Mandeb's small size and economic importance have made it a target for attacks. After the attacks on the USS *Cole* and the French tanker *Limburg*, security of the strait became a major concern, especially given its importance in the oil trade. Every day, 3.3 million barrels of Arabian oil pass through the Bab el-Mandeb on oil tankers, making it one of the busiest shipping lanes in the world.[3]

Yemen claims three major islands off its coasts. Perim lies in the Bab el-Mandeb, Kamaran in the Red Sea, and Socotra—the largest—in the Gulf of Aden.

Port of Aden

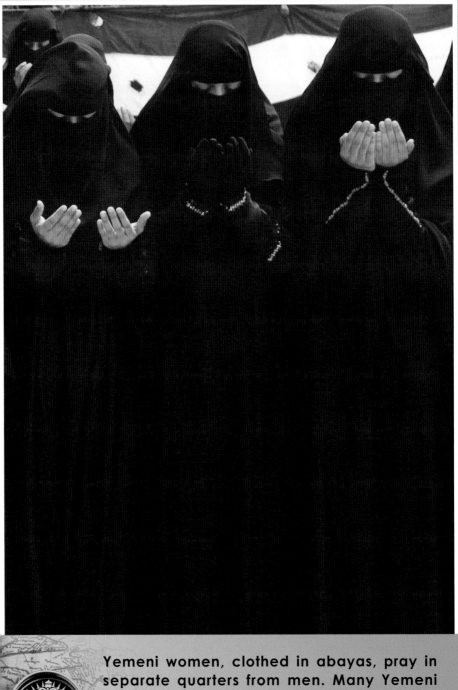

Yemeni women, clothed in abayas, pray in separate quarters from men. Many Yemeni women enjoy the privacy of the abaya. They consider it bad manners to show their faces to men other than their husbands.

To Be a Yemeni

Nearly all Yemenis are Arabs, with few immigrants from other countries. Most non-native Yemenis have moved there from Africa, especially Somalia, to escape war and violence.

The call to prayer rings out from every mosque in Yemen five times a day. Throughout cities and villages alike, Yemenis stop what they are doing and face Mecca to pray. *Islam* means "submission," specifically submission to the will of Allah, or God. Muslims believe that Allah's will was revealed through the angel Gabriel to the Prophet Muhammad, who recorded it in the Koran, Islam's holy book. Islam shares its history and some of its literature with Judaism and Christianity—religions that arose in the same part of the world. The Koran guides every aspect of Yemeni life, from holidays to literature to law. The Prophet himself once said of Yemen's people, "They have the kindest and gentlest hearts of all. Faith is Yemeni, wisdom is Yemeni."[1]

Muslims divide themselves into two major sects. Sunni Islam has the largest number of followers worldwide. Sunnis believe that any Muslim can become a religious or political leader. Over 99 percent of all Yemenis practice Islam, which is also the official state religion. Fifty-two percent of Yemenis are Shafi'i Muslims, a type of Sunni who believes that Muhammad dictated the Koran directly from Allah's words.[2] A large minority—45 percent—of Yemeni Muslims are Shi'ite, most belonging to the Zaydi sect.[3] In contrast to Sunnis, Shi'a Muslims believe that only descendants of the Prophet Muhammad are qualified to lead Allah's people. Further, the Zaydi Shi'ites believe that Muhammad used his human talents to craft the Koran's words—with Allah's inspiration. Though these differences in beliefs may seem small to outsiders, they lie at the heart of much of the political struggle and violence in the region since Muhammad's death in 632 CE.

For traditional Islamic countries like Yemen, Islam is not just a religion, it is also a way of life. Yemenis expect their laws, called shari'a, to do God's work as well. Shari'a is based on the Koran and the Hadith, which are collections of Muhammad's thoughts and works. It places high regard on modesty, honesty, fairness, and self-control. Shari'a laws include praying regularly, observing holy days, keeping women separate from men, and refraining from drinking alcohol or eating pork. In traditional Islamic countries, lawbreakers meet harsh punishment. Allah must be obeyed.

Shari'a can be interpreted to govern women's modesty, especially in public. Yemeni women and men are rarely seen in the same room in public, whether they are attending a mosque, a party, or even their own wedding. Before leaving the house, a typical Yemeni woman covers herself from head to toe in a flowing black over-cloth called an abaya. Many women also veil their face with a black cloth burka, so their entire body is covered except for their hands and eyes. Though some countries, such as Saudi Arabia, require women to dress this way by law, Yemen does not. In general, Yemeni women believe that dressing so modestly is simply good manners, and they appreciate the privacy of covering themselves. Women enjoy additional rights not found in many other Islamic states. In Yemen, for example, women can own property, drive, seek a divorce, vote, and run for political office.

Even so, women in Yemen live very different, and more restricted, lives than women in Western countries do. As soon as girls are old enough and strong enough, they are expected to cook and clean for the family, and to take care of the many younger children and babies in the house. Many girls drop out of school at an early age to help in this way. While many Yemenis acknowledge that education is important, household skills are viewed as much more practical for girls to learn. The average Yemeni mother bears seven children, meaning every household requires an army of skilled women—all family members—to

Yemeni women fill water jugs between the villages of Shuraijah and Karesh, south of Sana'a. Yemenis get their drinking water from pumps connected to aquifers deep underground. At the current rate of use, water resource experts estimate that Yemen's water supply could dry up by 2025.[4]

tend to their large family every day. Women in rural areas must additionally gather all the fuel—wood or animal dung—that the family will need for heating and cooking. They carry heavy water jugs to the nearest well or wadi and back home each day, sometimes over long distances.

As of 2011, the average life expectancy of a Yemeni was 63 years—66 years for females, 62 years for males. Less than 3 percent of the population lives beyond 65 years of age. Among Middle Eastern countries, only Afghanistan's life expectancy is lower. In comparison, Israel boasts the region's oldest residents, with an average life expectancy of 81 years. Additionally, Yemen's population is growing at an alarming rate—2.71 percent, one of the highest rates in the world.[5] Rapid growth makes for a young population; 44 percent of Yemenis are 14 years old or younger. Experts forecast that, as Yemen's youth reaches childbearing age, the population will double to 38.8 million by 2025.

Weddings play a major role in Yemeni social life. Families throw elaborate parties and get-togethers for several days before the actual event, with women celebrating separately from men. During this time, the couple signs a contract in front of an Islamic law official to make their marriage legal. The wedding ceremony takes place on the final day of celebration, usually a Friday. The men gather in the afternoon while the women cook a feast. In the evening, the men go to the mosque to pray, with the groom dressed in traditional clothes, a ceremonial golden sword slung from his belt. After prayers, the men sing and dance around the groom all the way to his house. Then they eat their feast, burning incense and saying blessings. After dinner, they chew qat, recite poetry, and sing songs accompanied by the oud (a traditional stringed instrument that is the precursor to the European lute).

Meanwhile, the women get ready at the bride's house, where a body painter dyes their hands and feet with intricate henna designs. The bride wears the finest possible clothes and jewelry.

When the bride and groom are ready, men line up outside the groom's house and sing. The groom strides past them and leaps over the doorstep. While everyone waits for the bride's father to bring her, the women climb onto the roof of the house and sing loudly. When she comes, the bride enters the groom's house, signifying that she has become part of his family.

Marriages in Yemen are arranged by parents, the custom among traditional Islamic families. Men may take up to four wives, as the Prophet Muhammad did. However, wives cost money; most Yemeni men can afford only one. The bride's father often receives a dowry—money, animals, or land from the groom's father. Though the average woman gets married at age eighteen, cash-strapped families have been known to offer up daughters as young as eight for marriage. Nujood Ali, a ten-year-old from Sana'a who divorced her thirty-year-old husband, horrified the world with her shocking tale of neglect and abuse, which was published and became a bestselling book (*I Am Nujood, Age 10 and Divorced*).[6] Government attempts to set the minimum age for marriage to seventeen and limit a dowry's size continue to be blocked by religious leaders.

Students read in an all-girls class at the Shaheed Mohamed Motaher Zaid School in Sana'a. Yemen's Social Fund for Development, sponsored by funds from the World Bank, supports this and other schools to improve education for Yemeni girls.

Language and Learning

Yemen's official language is Arabic, introduced to the region by Islam. People in Yemen communicate using three forms of Arabic. Classical Arabic is the written language of the Koran and is hundreds of years old. Modern Standard Arabic is the widely used version of Arabic, found in today's Arabic literature and newspapers. TV reporters, such as those on the all-Arab TV network Al-Jazeera, speak Modern Standard Arabic. Arabic speakers have their own regional dialects and accents, and sometimes it can be difficult for people from different parts of the country to understand each other. Yemenis regard their dialect as the most ancient, and therefore the purest, of all Arabic dialects.

Ancient Sabeans spoke a non-Arabic language that is more closely related to Hebrew. The Sabean language is still spoken by about 170,000 people, mainly in southern Yemen. Other languages spoken in Yemen—such as Soqotri, spoken by inhabitants of the island of Socotra; Mehri, spoken by 70,000 people in the far east; and Bathari, spoken by about 200 Yemenis—are similar to languages spoken by Yemen's African neighbors in Ethiopia and Eritrea.

The Yemen government's Ministry of Information controls the news that the public hears. TV and radio are especially important because of the many Yemenis who cannot read. Yemenis who can read can choose between the national newspaper, *Al-Thawra,* written in Arabic, and *Yemen Times,* written in English and available online. Reporters have been known to go to prison for writing stories that speak out against the government.

Historically, schools were only for the rich, leaving most of the impoverished country illiterate. Families especially discouraged their girls from attending school, partly for religious and modesty reasons. Today, only 60 percent of all children finish fifth grade; 48 percent of boys continue on to attend high school, but only 27 percent of girls do.[1] Once girls reach a helpful age, most families pull them out of school to help with the housework and child care. Yemen's constitution gives all citizens the right to an education, and even requires all chil-

Yemeni youth study the Koran inside the Grand Mosque of Sana'a's historical district. This mosque has educated Islam's faithful for over 1,200 years.

dren aged 6 to 15 to attend school, but the government does not enforce these laws.

Yemen is plagued with one of the largest literacy gender differences in the world. In 2007, 93 percent of young men could read, while only 67 percent of young women could. Yemenis pride themselves on a strong cultural tradition of poetry and memorization that make reading unnecessary. In the past, schools taught mostly memorization of the Koran. Even children who did not attend school were encouraged at home to memorize and recite poems and the Koran, and to compose their own poems. In Yemen, poetry is celebrated as a way to solve problems, manage differences, and express feelings. In a culture where modesty prevents men and women from socializing, poetry gives them a way to communicate with each other. Being able to recite poetry from memory is still highly respected throughout Yemeni society.

Yemen has a network of universities in Aden, Hudaydah, Ibb, Ta'izz, Hadramawt, and Dhamar. These universities began as extensions of Sana'a University. Established in 1970, it was the first organized university in Yemen, and it is still recognized as the country's premiere university, enrolling up to 14,000 students each year. Other community colleges, technical schools, and teacher-training schools serve education needs throughout the country. College admissions and hiring usually favor men over women, but increasing numbers of women find their way onto college campuses and into the workplace.

FYI FACT:

Some Arabic phrases include:

As-salaamu 'aleykum: Peace be upon you (meaning, Hi!)

Wa 'aleykum as-salaam: And upon you be peace (Hi back!)

Ana isimi . . . : My name is . . .

Kayf haluka (male)/ *Kayf haluki* (female): How are you?

Insha'allah: If Allah wills it[2]

An elderly woman sits inside her mud-reed house in the Tihama. Yemenis build with mud from the local wadi to make simple, practical homes that provide natural insulation from the desert heat.

Chapter 7

Family, Food, and Fun

In Yemen, family is extremely important. Many generations of families live together in a single house. Housing styles throughout the country reflect this lifestyle, though materials vary according to region. Homes in the coastal Tihama are built from mud-covered reeds and sticks, fenced by stone or mud walls. In the wadis of the east, people prefer Indian building styles, adopted during British rule, that rely on hand-made sun-dried bricks. Many homes link together several one-room buildings, each with a specific purpose, such as kitchen or bedroom. In the highlands, Yemenis build stone or clay houses that are seven or eight stories tall and decorated with colored glass, carved wood, and alabaster. Lower levels are used for stables and storage. One large room, the *diwan,* is reserved for parties. On the top floor is the *matraj,* a special room where the owner formally greets his guests, and where men gather to chew qat and talk away from the women.

Yemenis love to eat big meals together. Visit a Yemeni household—especially at lunch, the main meal—and dishes piled high with thick, spicy stews, fresh baked bread, and dates with honey will appear before your eyes. Popular dishes include *ful,* a stew eaten for any meal. It is made from fava beans, onions, tomatoes, and chili peppers. *Salta* is a thick spicy stew with vegetables and

Salta

41

Imam Yahya entertained friends and special guests in this elaborate *diwan*, or meeting room, in the Dhar al-Hajar. The imam built his famous five-story rock palace as a summer home just outside of Sana'a in the 1930s.

lamb or chicken served over bread or rice. Warm bread, a favorite part of every meal, is often used instead of forks and spoons to scoop up food. Yemenis drink hot, sweet tea all day long. The original coffee capital of the world prefers its coffee powdered and boiled with sugar and ginger, a drink called *qishr*. Yemenis do not care much for sweets, with the notable exception of honey. Yemeni honey, particularly from the Wadi Hadramawt region, is considered an international delicacy.

Yemenis are poets at heart; they love to listen to poetry as well as create their own. Books are not very popular in Yemen, but memorized and recited poetry makes for a valuable entertainment form. Popular

IRAN
Ahvāz
sirīyah
Ahādān
Kermān

Family, Food, and Fun

7

topics celebrate special occasions like marriage, holidays, politics, or nothing at all. Yemen's most famous poet, Abdullah al-Baradouni (1929–1999) wrote poetry in support of democracy and women's rights. Sayyid Ahmad Zabara (1908–2000), a religious leader, wrote a famous collection of 360 poems that told of Yemeni history. Without question, the most popular poems are verses from the Koran.

When Yemenis set their poetry to music, they favor traditional sounds and instruments. In the cities, musicians play the *kabanj,* a stringed lute, and two small drums. A wind instrument with a double reed known as a *mizmar* is enjoyed in the quiet music of the highlands. Ayoob Tarish Absi is a famous Yemeni musician known as Yemen's *Bulbul,* or songbird. He plays the oud and sings traditional songs celebrating love for Yemen and for Allah. He composed Yemen's national anthem, "United Republic."

Yemen has few professional artists or art schools, since the country is too poor for artists to make a living selling their work. Instead, most Yemeni art takes a practical form. Beautiful geometric designs decorate houses and mosques. Calligraphy, an artistic form of handwriting, is a popular way to illustrate the Koran. Artisans embellish the bone or ivory handles of the *jambiya* with intricate carved designs. Craftspeople in souks sell their handmade silver jewelry; woven clothing, rugs, and baskets; and handmade wooden boxes.

Football (soccer) is easily Yemen's most popular sport. Yemen's national team competes with other teams worldwide through the international soccer organization FIFA. Boxing is also a favorite sport among Yemeni men. One of Yemen's favorite sons is world champion boxer Naseem "The Prince" Hamed, born and raised in the United Kingdom to Yemeni parents. Organized sports are becoming popular in cities, where more Yemenis have money for equipment or training.

Mizmar

Holidays in Yemen celebrate both secular and religious events. Islam follows the lunar calendar, counting years beginning with Muhammad's journey in 622 CE from Mecca to Medina in Saudi Arabia. This journey, called the hegira, is celebrated as the Muslim New Year, on Muharram 1. Yemenis also celebrate Muhammad's birthday. A three-day-long festival commemorates Eid al-Adha, the Feast of Sacrifice that remembers how Ibrahim (or Abraham) sacrificed a ram in place of his son Ishmael (not Isaac, as in the Old Testament of the Bible). Families who can afford it slaughter a sheep, feast on about one-third of the meat, and share the rest with the poor.

During the holy month of Ramadan, when Muhammad became Allah's prophet, Islam dictates that its followers not eat or drink between sunrise and sunset. In Yemen, the entire country slows down to

Yemeni craftspeople sell handmade wares such as these colorful woven baskets at city market places called souks.

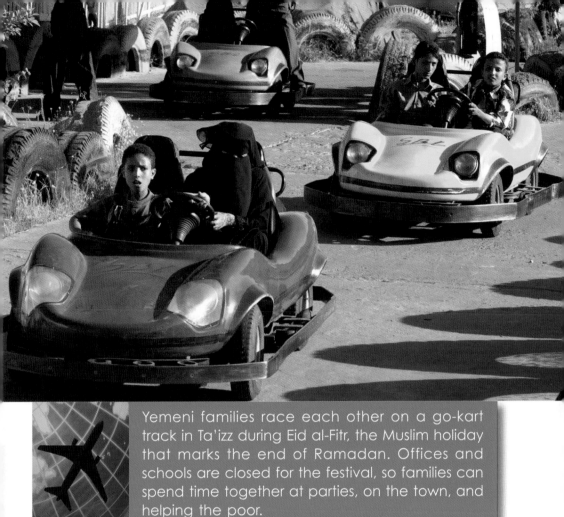

Yemeni families race each other on a go-kart track in Ta'izz during Eid al-Fitr, the Muslim holiday that marks the end of Ramadan. Offices and schools are closed for the festival, so families can spend time together at parties, on the town, and helping the poor.

observe Ramadan, especially during the day, as people spend time praying or resting at home. Ramadan's nights bring people spilling out into the streets to laugh, talk, and eat together. The holy month ends with Eid al-Fitr, two days of feasts and worship. During this time, Yemenis buy new clothes, clean their homes, and visit friends and family.

Secular holidays follow a solar calendar. May 22 is the Day of National Unity, commemorating the unification of the two Yemens into the Republic of Yemen in 1990. September 26 is Revolution Day, commemorating the 1962 overthrow of Zaydi imams in northern Yemen. In remembrance of the liberation of South Yemen from British rule, Yemenis also celebrate October 14 as National Day and November 30 as Independence Day.

A Yemeni qat seller samples his wares. Many Yemenis, especially men, chew the leaves of this stimulant drug. Qat is illegal in most countries.

Chapter

8

Jobs in Yemen

Yemen's rich land made it possible for its ancient people to live as farmers and traders, while Arabians in other areas wandered the desert as nomads. In modern times, neighboring Arabic countries have grown wealthy from oil, but little has changed in Yemen.

More than half of Yemen's population works on farms. Many families live together in small villages, where they herd goats, sheep, and some cattle. Those who wish to try their hand at taming the mountain soil make terraces to farm crops. Unfortunately, because of desertification and a water shortage of crisis proportions, only 2.9 percent of Yemen's land can be farmed, and less than 0.3 percent is permanently farmed.[1] Nearly all fertile land is found in the western mountains or in wadis. Yemeni farmers grow grains; vegetables; grapes, figs, bananas, mangoes, papayas, and other fruit; cotton; and coffee. "Mocha" coffee originates from the Yemeni city of Mokha, home of the coffee trade. In the central highlands, farmers grow fruit trees such as pear, apricot, pomegranate, and date; and nut trees such as almond and walnut. Myrrh and the fragrant sap of frankincense—upon which wealthy kingdoms were built—are still harvested from the scraggly plants that cling to rocks in the mountains. Fishermen make a living in port cities using mainly small boats, poles, and nets to bring in their catch.[2]

Yemen's most valuable crop is qat, a small evergreen tree with broad leaves. Though many countries have outlawed qat as an illegal drug, chewing qat leaves plays a major role in Yemeni culture. Yemeni men

Farming in Yemen

often meet in the afternoons to chew qat and talk for hours. Formal qat chews are a time to discuss business transactions and arrange marriages.[3]

While most Yemenis view qat use as beneficial, it negatively impacts family life and the country's economy. Time spent chewing takes time away from jobs and families. Qat fans are quick to point out that qat is farmed in Yemen, so their money goes to support Yemeni farmers. However, qat's critics point out that qat farms take over 40 percent of the nation's water supply to produce a crop that has no nutritional value. And at $10 per bunch, high-end users easily spend half their family's already thin income on their habit. President Saleh quit his qat habit to set an example for other men.

In 2011, less than 25 percent of Yemenis were employed in industry, services, or business,[4] though much of Yemen's money is made in manufacturing, mining, and construction. Before the revolutions that created North and South Yemen, industrial growth was limited by a lack of money, roads, and training. After the revolutions, foreign powers sank money into the country and built factories to make soft drinks, cigarettes, cloth, small aluminum products, and food products.

In the 1980s, U.S. energy companies discovered oil deposits in the highlands of western central Yemen. By 1986, five wells were pumping near Marib, delivering oil via newly built pipelines to the port city of Hudaydah on the Red Sea. By 1989, Yemen's oil fields were producing over 200,000 barrels per day. Oil engineers estimate that Yemen sits on 2.7 billion barrels of oil in proven reserves,[5] quite low for the region but a resource nonetheless. The Yemeni government is working fever-ishly to recruit foreign investors and further develop its oil resources, with the goal of boosting output to 400,000 barrels per day. Progress is slow, however, as the oil reserves are located in a rugged area where roads are difficult to build. Meanwhile, oil refineries in Hudaydah and Aden find extra work refining oil from other countries. Yemen makes due with its plentiful reserves of natural gas, supplying its own power stations to generate cheap electricity for its people.

In 2009, the average income per person was about 212,000 Yemeni rials, or about US$1,060.[6] Yemenis are by far the poorest people in the Middle East; in the rest of the region, oil revenues help boost the aver-age income to US$6,105.[7] Yemenis are even slightly poorer than their neighbors in impoverished African countries across the Red Sea. Many Yemenis rely on money sent home from relatives working overseas. Around 25 percent of Yemenis, especially young males, seek unskilled jobs in Saudi Arabia and the UAE, or more ambitious positions in Europe and the United States. Money sent home from these overseas workers is a disturbingly important source of income for many families.

Most of Yemen's financial problems come from poor money man-agement by the government. The Yemeni government is the country's largest employer, and 80 percent of its revenues come from oil money.[8] Because of the difficulties obtaining Yemeni oil, and its poor outlook for the future, the entire economy is on shaky ground. Yemen relies heavily on financial assistance from foreign powers. The World Bank sponsors 19 projects in Yemen, using the money to improve the govern-ment, water supply and quality, and education. Saleh's government was also seeking ways to diversify its income by expanding agriculture, historically a major source of income for Yemen. The government would like to attract foreign companies to do business in Yemen, but because of terrorist attacks and violence by Houthi rebels in the north, companies are unwilling to invest in the region.

The bottle tree (*Adenium obesum*) survives the dry climate on Socotra Island by storing water in its trunk. The tree bursts into pink blooms before the rainy season, giving it the nickname "desert rose."

We Visit Yemen

Tucked away like a secret in the southwest corner of the Arabian Peninsula, the Republic of Yemen has much to offer tourists seeking adventure. An old saying in Yemen urges: "Sana'a must be seen, however long the journey or how low the camel droops on knotted knee." Spectacular archaeological digs are ongoing in Marib and Zabid. The Gulf of Aden boasts some of the most beautiful beaches in the region. And the strange and beautiful island of Socotra, off the south coast, plays host to migrating sea turtle populations, coral reefs, and native plants and animals that are found nowhere else in the world. With its rich history and unspoiled landscapes, Yemen hopes to build a reputation as an international tourist destination.

A journey to Yemen usually begins and ends in Sana'a, the largest city. This world treasure is quite possibly the oldest continuously inhabited city in the world. Sana'a is famous for its medina, an old walled section of the city that dates back to the first century CE. Built of brick, mud, and stone, many houses in the medina are more than 400 years old. The buildings are decorated so ornately with white gypsum that they look like a gingerbread village. Among the tall roofs of the medina buildings—many seven stories high—rise the elaborate minarets of the mosques. Al-Jami al-Kabir, the largest mosque in Sana'a, houses fountains and many buildings within its walls. Also inside the medina is Sana'a's famous Souk al Milh, an open-air market where vendors sell produce, qat, spices, and crafts. Sana'a's age and importance to world history has led the United Nations to declare the

 The al-Saleh Mosque in Sana'a opened to worshipers during Ramadan in 2008. Yemeni craftsmen built the architectural masterpiece out of mostly local materials. President Saleh personally paid for the construction of the $60 million mosque.

old walled city a World Heritage Site. This designation brings with it money dedicated to maintaining and restoring the historic buildings.

Just thirty minutes' drive from Sana'a is the scenic Wadi Dhar, home to Dhar al-Hajar, or Rock Palace. Built by Imam Yahya as a summer home in the 1930s, the house stands atop a rock formation that vaults it above the scenery.

Called the Manhattan of the Desert, the ancient walled city of Shibam was built by the Hadramawt kingdom to keep out Bedouin invaders. The Hadramawts built skyscraper apartment buildings out of mud bricks over 500 years ago. Today, they stand as the tallest mud buildings in the world, earning Shibam its place as a UNESCO World Heritage Site. The nearby town of Tarim boasts the tallest mud-brick structure in the world, a minaret that rises 175 feet.

Marib (population 4,000) in west-central Yemen is the site of the capital of the ancient kingdom of Saba. The fabled Queen of Sheba

Imam Yahya built Dhar al-Hajar on a tall rock formation. He was not the first to build on this unlikely site. A prehistoric well and building ruins were already there when construction began.

possibly called Marib her home. Because of the ancient treasures found there, Marib is one of the most archaeologically important sites in Yemen.

Aden (population 800,000) sits in the crater of an extinct volcano. As the country's main port, Aden is the economic center of the country, and was the capital of the People's Democratic Republic of Yemen. Its strategic location at the corner of the Red Sea and the Gulf of Aden has made it a hub for seagoing trade since ancient times. Today, foreign ships stop in Aden's port to refuel for their journey through the Red Sea and the Suez Canal, or across the Indian Ocean. Yemen ships fish, coffee, tobacco, cotton, and salt for export to other countries. Aden additionally boasts the country's biggest international airport and modern roads—a rare luxury in Yemen. Compared to other Yemeni cities, Aden attracts a multicultural population. The city swelled with Arabic soccer fans when it hosted the 20th Gulf Cup tournament in November and December 2010.

Ta'izz (population 460,000) in the southwest is positively young compared to other Yemeni cities, dating back to the seventh century CE. Beautiful Ta'izz boasts ancient souks and mosques as well as the modern conveniences of a big city, all at the foot of the scenic Saber Mountain. It has famous mosques and souks, as well as modern neighborhoods.

Can you stand the Tihama's heat? Journey along the Red Sea to see charming port towns. Learn the craft of ancient shipbuilding in Al-Khokha village, or visit Hudaydah (population 400,000), a port on the Red Sea. After a terrible fire destroyed much of the city in 1961, it was rebuilt with help from the Soviet Union. The port especially was expanded and improved.

The island of Socotra is Yemen's hidden treasure. Over 700 unique plant and animal species call Socotra home, making it second only to Hawaii for ecological richness. Besides the migrating sea turtles, the island serves as a host to dozens of species of birds, and it is a special favorite of the Egyptian vulture. Socotra's most famous native species is the Dragon's Blood tree, which stands like an inside-out umbrella of dark evergreen. The people of Socotra (population 40,000) live a quiet life of fishing and herding.

The strange and beautiful Dragon's Blood tree grows only on a handful of islands in the Socotra Archipelago. The dark red sap of this evergreen tree has many uses, from paints to medicines and toothpaste.

Yemen is a land that seems frozen in time, a unique opportunity in the modern world to experience the ancient. But to the traveler, Yemen's greatest gift is its people. Despite their poverty and hardships, Yemenis are known for their easygoing hospitality, and they rarely refuse a request for help. They also love to talk, enjoying lengthy, casual conversations with strangers as well as good friends. Yemenis insist on a slow pace of life, which gives them time to enjoy their family, friends, and helping others. Take a load off from a busy life and make some new friends in Yemen!

Yemeni Fatah

Yemen's favorite dishes are thick and filling stews like this lamb *fatah*. Instead of forks and spoons, use warm pita or naan bread to scoop the hot *fatah* for an authentic Yemeni experience!

Ingredients
1 tablespoon oil
1 large onion, halved lengthwise and sliced crosswise
    (1 heaping cup)
1 large clove garlic, minced
¾ pound lean lamb, cut into thin 2-inch-long strips
½ cup beef broth
¼ teaspoon oregano
¼ teaspoon cumin
¼ teaspoon coriander
⅛ teaspoon allspice, salt and pepper to taste
1 cup couscous, cooked according to package directions
2 tablespoons minced fresh parsley

Directions
1. In a medium skillet, heat the oil, then sauté the onion and garlic until the onion is translucent.
2. Add the lamb. Sauté the meat, stirring it often, just until it is brown on all sides.
3. Stir in the broth, oregano, cumin, coriander, allspice, salt, and pepper, and cook the mixture a few minutes longer.
4. Spread the cooked couscous on a platter.
5. Spoon the meat mixture over the couscous and sprinkle with parsley.

Yemeni Mud Bricks

From the walled city of Shibam to the medina of Sana'a, mud bricks are a vital component of Yemeni buildings. They are inexpensive, fireproof, and perfect for the dry climate of Yemen. Build your own ancient city with these toy-sized mud bricks.

You will need
dirt (preferably dug—ask permission first)
sieve or mesh screen
water
large mixing bowl
shredded newspaper
ice cube trays
spoon
flat tray or baking sheet

Instructions
1. Sift the dirt through the sieve to remove pebbles. Add the sifted dirt to the mixing bowl.
2. Mix the dirt, with a spoon or your hands, with enough water to make thick mud. If your mixture seems soupy, add more dirt. Sprinkle some shredded newspaper into the mixture to give the final bricks strength.
3. With a spoon, scoop the mud mixture into the ice cube trays, filling each compartment. Let the mud dry overnight.
4. Turn the bricks out onto a tray or baking sheet and set them in the sun for a few days to dry completely. Enjoy your new bricks!

1500s	Yemen becomes part of the Ottoman Empire.
1839	Aden comes under British rule.
1869	Suez Canal opens; Aden becomes a major refueling port.
1918	Ottoman Empire falls. North Yemen gains independence, with Imam Yahya as ruler.
1948	Yahya is assassinated on February 17, and his son Ahmad becomes ruler.
1962	Imam Ahmad dies and is succeeded by his son. In a coup, the army sets up the Yemen Arab Republic (YAR), sparking civil war.
1967	Southern Yemen forms on November 30, comprising Aden and former Protectorate of South Arabia. This country is later officially known as the People's Democratic Republic of Yemen (PDRY).
1978	Ali Abdullah Saleh becomes president of YAR.
1982	An earthquake near Dhamar, North Yemen kills 2,800 people in December.
1990	North and South Yemen become the unified Republic of Yemen, with Saleh as president.
1991	Yemen opposes U.S.-led action against Iraq in Gulf War.
1994	Relations between southern and northern leaders sour. On May 21, Al-Baid declares independence of Democratic Republic of Yemen, but secession is declared illegal. In July, northern forces take control of Aden. Secessionist leaders flee.
2000	The USS *Cole* is damaged in an al-Qaeda attack in Aden on October 12, killing 17 U.S. sailors. A bomb explodes at the British embassy.
2001	After the terrorist attacks on U.S. soil on September 11, President Saleh visits the United States, telling President George W. Bush that Yemen will be a partner in the fight against terrorism.
2002	The French oil tanker *Limburg* is badly damaged off the Yemeni coast on October 16 in an attack that is blamed on al-Qaeda.
2004	Government troops battle supporters of Hussein al-Houthi; estimates of the dead range from 80 to more than 600. Al-Houthi is reportedly killed in September.
2005	More than 200 people are killed in a resurgence of fighting between government forces and supporters of al-Houthi.
2006	President Saleh wins another term in the September 20th elections.
2007	Rebel leader Abdul-Malik al-Houthi accepts a ceasefire. A suicide bomber attacks a tourist convoy on July 2, killing eight. On September 30, a volcano erupts on Jabal al-Tair, an island where Yemen has a military base.
2008	Security forces and rebels loyal to Abdul-Malik al-Houthi battle in the north. Rebels target police, officials, foreign businesses, and tourists with bombs. The U.S. embassy evacuates all non-essential personnel. In September, the U.S. embassy in Sana'a is attacked, and 18 people, including six terrorists, are killed.
2009	Yemen releases 176 al-Qaeda suspects for good behavior while behind bars. The Yemeni army launches a fresh offensive against Shi'a rebels in the northern Sa'ada province. Tens of thousands of people are displaced by the fighting. Al-Qaeda in Yemen takes credit for a failed December 25 attack on a U.S. airliner.
2010	The government signs a ceasefire with northern rebels on February 12.
2011	U.S. Secretary of State Hillary Clinton visits to express "urgent concern" about al-Qaeda activities in Yemen. In response to nationwide protests throughout the spring, President Saleh pledges to step down as president.

Chapter 1. Yemen, Ancient and Beautiful

1. Daniel McLaughlin, *Yemen* (Bucks, U.K.: Bradt Travel Guides, 2007), p.vii.
2. U.S. Central Intelligence Agency, *World Factbook:* "Yemen." November 4, 2010, https://www.cia.gov/library/publications/the-world-factbook/geos/ym.html

Chapter 2. The History of "Arabia Felix"

1. Remy Crassard, "Modalities and Characteristics of Human Occupations in Yemen During the Early/Mid Holocene," *Comptes Rendus Geosciences,* July/August 2009, Volume 341, Issues 8–9, p. 715.
2. The Bible, 1 Kings 10; The Koran, 34th chapter.
3. Rhea Talley Stewart, "A Dam at Marib," *Saudi Aramco World,* March/April 1978, vol. 29, no. 2, pp. 24–29.

Chapter 3. Government

1. IFES Election Guide, "Country Profile: Yemen," http://www.electionguide.org/country.php?ID=1039
2. Ibid.
3. Iris Glosemeyer, "Dancing on Snake Heads in Yemen," The Canadian Defence and Foreign Affairs Institute, May 2009, http://www.cdfai.org/PDF/Dancing%20on%20Snake%20Heads%20in%20Yemen.pdf

Chapter 4. Hot Lands and the Roof of Arabia

1. Daniel McLaughlin, *Yemen* (Bucks, U.K.: Bradt Travel Guides), 2007, p. 165.
2. World Heritage Convention, "Historic Town of Zabid," http://whc.unesco.org/en/list/611/
3. U.S. Energy Information Administration, "World Oil Transit Chokepoints," January 2008, http://www.eia.doe.gov/cabs/World_Oil_Transit_Chokepoints/Full.html

Chapter 5. To Be a Yemeni

1. Tim Mackintosh-Smith, *Yemen: The Unknown Arabia* (Woodstock, NY: The Overlook Press, 2000), p. ix.
2. Bobby Ghosh and Oliver Holmes, "Al Qaeda's Magazine in Yemen: Where's Our Wikileaks Scoop?" *Time,* November 30, 2010. http://www.time.com/time/world/article/0,8599,2033638,00.html
3. Ibid.
4. "Sana'a Faces 2017 Water Crunch," *Middle East Online,* March 24, 2010, http://middle-east-online.com/english/?id=38032
5. United Nations Development Programme, "Yemen," http://www.undp.org.ye
6. Nujood Ali and Delphine Minoui, *I Am Nujood, Age 10 and Divorced* (New York: Three Rivers Press, 2010).

Chapter 6. Language and Learning

1. UNICEF, "At a Glance: Yemen—Statistics," http://www.unicef.org/infobycountry/yemen_statistics.html
2. Virtual Tourist: Arabic Phrasebook http://members.virtualtourist.com/m/tt/15070/

Chapter 8. Jobs in Yemen

1. U.S. Central Intelligence Agency, *World Factbook:* "Yemen," November 4, 2010, https://www.cia.gov/library/publications/the-world-factbook/geos/ym.html
2. Ministry of Planning and International Cooperation, "State of the Yemeni Economy (2003)," http://www.mpic-yemen.org/new1/new_containt.asp?contantmain=7&key=19
3. Jennifer Steil, *The Woman Who Fell From the Sky: Adventures in the Oldest City on Earth* (New York: Broadway Books, 2010), p. 246.
4. Congressional Quarterly Inc., *The Middle East,* 10th Edition (Washington, DC: CQ Press, 2005), p. 422.

ISRAEL

Alexandria

Port Jerusalem — West Bank'D E S E R T

Said ★Amman

Cairo Suez Canal Gaza Strip Dead Sea (lowest point in Asia, -408 m)

JORDAN

I

5. British Petroleum, "Statistical Review of World Energy, June 2010," http://www.bp.com/liveassets/bp_internet/globalbp/globalbp_uk_english/reports_and_publications/statistical_energy_review_2008/STAGING/local_assets/2010_downloads/statistical_review_of_world_energy_full_report_2010.pdf

6. The World Bank, "Republic of Yemen," 2009, http://data.worldbank.org/country/yemen-republic

7. The World Bank, "The Middle East," 2009, http://data.worldbank.org/country/ZQ

8. Melissa Roussi, *What Every American Should Know About the Middle East* (New York: Penguin Group, 2008).

FURTHER READING

Books

DiPiazza, Francesca Davis. *Yemen in Pictures.* Minneapolis: Lerner Publishing Group, 2008.

Hestler, Anna, and JoAnn Spilling. *Yemen.* Tarrytown, NY: Marshall Cavendish Children's Books, 2010.

Marcovitz, Hal. *Yemen.* Philadelphia: Mason Crest Publishers, 2009.

Sonnenborn, Liz. *Yemen: Enchantment of the World.* New York: Scholastic, 2008.

Works Consulted

Ali, Nujood, and Delphine Minoui. *I Am Nujood, Age 10 and Divorced.* New York: Three Rivers Press, 2010.

BBC Monitoring. "Yemen Country Profile." *BBC News,* updated March 17, 2010. http://news.bbc.co.uk/2/hi/middle_east/country_profiles/784383.stm

British Petroleum. "Statistical Review of World Energy, June 2010." http://www.bp.com/liveassets/bp_internet/globalbp/globalbp_uk_english/reports_and_publications/statistical_energy_review_2008/STAGING/local_assets/2010_downloads/statistical_review_of_world_energy_full_report_2010.pdf

Burdick, Alan. "The Wonder Land of Socotra." *The New York Times,* March 25, 2007. http://travel.nytimes.com/2007/03/25/travel/tmagazine/03well.socotra.t.html

Caton, Steven C. *Yemen Chronicle: An Anthropology of War and Mediation.* New York: Hill and Wang, 2005.

Congressional Quarterly, Inc. *The Middle East.* 10th Edition. Washington, DC: CQ Press, 2005.

Crassard, Remy. "Modalities and Characteristics of Human Occupations in Yemen During the Early/Mid Holocene." *Comptes Rendus Geoscience.* July/August 2009, Volume 341, Issues 8–9, pp. 713–725.

Cronin, Audrey Kurth. "Terrorist Attacks by Al Qaeda." Congressional Research Service, memorandum, March 31, 2004. http://www.fas.org/irp/crs/033104.pdf

Frysinger, Galen. "Travel Photos of Hodeidah." http://www.galenfrysinger.com/hodeidah.htm

Ghosh, Bobby, and Oliver Holmes. "Al Qaeda's Magazine in Yemen: Where's Our Wikileaks Scoop?" *Time,* November 30, 2010. http://www.time.com/time/world/article/0,8599,2033638,00.html

Glosemeyer, Iris. "Dancing on Snake Heads in Yemen." The Canadian Defence and Foreign Affairs Institute, May 2009. http://www.cdfai.org/PDF/Dancing%20on%20Snake%20Heads%20in%20Yemen.pdf

Kasinof, Laura, and David E. Sanger. "U.S. Shifts to Seek Removal of Yemen's Leader, an Ally." *The New York Times,* April 3, 2011. http://www.nytimes.com/2011/04/04/world/middleeast/04yemen.html?pagewanted=2&_r=1&hp

Levy, Faye. *Feast from the Mideast.* New York: HarperCollins, 2003. http://www.inmamaskitchen.com/RECIPES/RECIPES/Breads/Yemenite_Kubaneh_overnight.html

Lonely Planet. "Yemen Travel Information and Travel Guide." Updated June 16, 2009. http://www.lonelyplanet.com/yemen

Mackintosh-Smith, Tim. *Yemen: The Unknown Arabia.* Woodstock, NY: The Overlook Press, 2000.

McLaughlin, Daniel. *Yemen.* Bucks, UK: Bradt Travel Guides, 2007.

Ministry of Planning and International Cooperation. "State of the Yemeni Economy (2003)." http://www.mpic-yemen.org/new1/new_containt.asp?contantmain=7&key=19

Rossi, Melissa. *What Every American Should Know About the Middle East.* New York: Penguin Group, 2008.

"Sana'a Faces 2017 Water Crunch." *Middle East Online,* March 24, 2010. http://www.middle-east-online.com/english/?id=38032

Steil, Jennifer. *The Woman Who Fell From the Sky: Adventures in the Oldest City on Earth.* New York: Broadway Books, 2010.

Stewart, Rhea Talley. "A Dam at Marib." *Saudi Aramco World,* March/April 1978, vol. 29, no. 2, pp. 24–29.

Sykes, Hugh. "The Dark Side of Children's Lives in Yemen." *BBC News,* January 30, 2010. http://news.bbc.co.uk/2/hi/programmes/from_our_own_correspondent/8487346.stm

Tharoor, Ishaan. "A Brief History of Yemen: Rich Past, Impoverished Present." *Time,* November 1, 2010. http://www.time.com/time/world/article/0,8599,2028740,00.html

On the Internet

BBC News: Yemen—Timeline http://news.bbc.co.uk/2/hi/middle_east/country_profiles/1706450.stm

The Embassy of the Republic of Yemen http://www.yemenembassy.org/

IFES Election Guide: "Country Profile: Yemen" http://www.electionguide.org/country.php?ID=237

The New York Times: Yemen News http://topics.nytimes.com/top/news/international/countriesandterritories/yemen/index.html

U.S. Central Intelligence Agency: *World Factbook:* "Yemen," https://www.cia.gov/library/publications/the-world-factbook/geos/ym.html

U.S. Department of State: "Travel Warning: Yemen" http://travel.state.gov/travel/cis_pa_tw/tw/tw_5364.html

U.S. Energy Information Administration: "World Oil Transit Chokepoints," January 2008. http://www.eia.doe.gov/cabs/World_Oil_Transit_Chokepoints/Full.html

World Heritage Convention: "Historic Town of Zabid" http://whc.unesco.org/en/list/611/

Yemen Times http://www.yementimes.com/

Yemen Tourism http://www.yementourism.com/

PHOTO CREDITS: Cover, pp. 2, 3, 8, 10–11, 15, 16–17, 23, 24, 25, 26, 27, 28–29, 30, 36, 40, 41, 44, 46, 48, 50, 52, 53, 55, 56, 57—cc-by-sa; pp. 1, 6–7—Photos.com/Getty Images; p. 14—Frans Francken II; p. 18—Grigory Gagarin; p. 19—Marcel Mettelsiefen/Getty Images; p. 22—AP Photo; pp. 33, 45—Khaled Fazaa/AFP/Getty Images; p. 38—Marwan Naamani/AFP/Getty Images; p. 42—David Rich. Every effort has been made to locate all copyright holders of material used in this book. If any errors or omissions have occurred, corrections will be made in future editions of the book.

GLOSSARY

abaya (uh-BY-uh)—A flowing black robe worn by Arabic women, usually with a headscarf and veil.

burka (BUR-kuh)—A loose, long-sleeved robe worn by traditional Muslim women that covers the entire body and face, with a slit or see-through veil for the eyes.

caliphate (KAL-ih-fayt)—A government headed by an Islamic leader, or caliph.

desalination (dee-sal-ih-NAY-shun)—The process of removing salt from saltwater in order to make it drinkable.

Gulf Cooperation Council—A group of Persian Gulf countries dominated by Saudi Arabia that also includes Oman, Bahrain, Qatar, Kuwait, and the United Arab Emirates.

Hadith (hah-DEETH)—A collection of legends about the prophet Muhammad and his followers.

hegira (hih-JY-ruh)—The flight of Muhammad from Mecca to Medina in 622 CE. The Muslim calendar begins in that year.

imam (ee-MAHM)—A Muslim religious leader.

Koran (kor-AN)—The holy book of Islam, believed to be the words of Allah as spoken to his prophet Muhammad.

mujahideen (moo-jah-hih-DEEN)—Muslim guerrilla fighters.

oud (OOD)—A traditional stringed instrument.

protectorate (proh-TEK-tur-ut)—A government set up within one country under the supervision of a stronger country.

qat (KAHT)—An evergreen shrub (*Catha edulis*) native to Africa and Arabia. Its leaves are chewed as a stimulant drug.

Shafi'i (SHAF-ee-ee)—One of four sects of Sunni Islam, founded by Abu Abdullah Muhammad ibn Idris al-Shafi'i (767–819 CE).

Shari'a (SHAH-ree-ah)—Islamic law, defined by how Muslim scholars interpret the Koran, the Hadith, and other sources.

sheik (SHAYK)—A leader of an Arabic community

Shi'ite (SHEE-eyt)—A follower of Shi'a Islam, which believes that true Islamic religious leaders must be descended from the Prophet Muhammad.

shura (SHOO-rah)—A council of Islamic scholars that makes official decisions in government and/or law.

Sunni (SOO-nee)—A follower of Sunni Islam, which believes that Islamic religious leaders need not be direct descendants of the Prophet Muhammad, but rather can be chosen by the *shura*.

UNESCO (yoo-NES-koh)— United Nations Educational, Scientific and Cultural Organization. A group within the United Nations that promotes and preserves goods and natural resources around the globe.

UNICEF (YOO-nih-sef)—United Nations Children's Fund. A group within the United Nations that works to feed, educate, and provide medical care to the world's children, especially in developing countries.

wadi (WAH-dee)—A riverbed carved by rainy-season floods that is dry most of the year.

Zaydi (ZAY-dee)—A moderate sect of Shi'a Islam.

Claire O'Neal has written over a dozen books for Mitchell Lane Publishers, including *We Visit Iraq* from this series. She holds degrees in English and Biology from Indiana University, and a Ph.D. in Chemistry from the University of Washington. She enjoys traveling, and internationally has visited Great Britain and New Zealand. She lives in Delaware with her husband and two young boys.